I'M GOOD AT ICT

WHAT JOB CAN I GET?

Richard Spilsbury

WAYLAND

First published in 2011 by Wayland
Copyright Wayland 2011

Wayland
Hachette Children's Books
338 Euston Road
London NW1 3BH

Wayland Australia
Level 17/207 Kent Street,
Sydney, NSW 2000

Commissioning editor: Camilla Lloyd
Project editor: Kelly Davis
Designer: Tim Mayer, MayerMedia
Picture research: Richard Spilsbury/Amy Sparks
Proofreader and indexer: Alice Harman

Produced for Wayland by
White-Thomson Publishing Ltd
www.wtpub.co.uk
+44 (0)843 2087 460

British Library Cataloguing in Publication Data

Spilsbury, Richard, 1963-
I'm good at – what job can I get?.
ICT.
1. Information technology–Vocational guidance–
Juvenile literature.
I. Title
004'.023-dc22

ISBN: 9780750265768

Printed in China

Wayland is a division of Hachette Children's Books, an Hachette UK company
www.hachette.co.uk

Picture credits

1, Dreamstime/Aniram; 3, Dreamstime/Danieloizo; 4, Shutterstock/Stavchansky Yakov; 5, Shutterstock/DMSU; 6, Dreamstime/Vling; 7, Shutterstock/Goodluz; 8, Dreamstime/Yuri_arcurs; 9, Dreamstime/Paha; 10, Dreamstime/Endostock; 11, Dreamstime/Razvanjp; 12, Dreamstime/Otnaydur; 13 (top), Dreamstime/Antares614; 13 (second down), Dreamstime/Markwaters; 13 (third down), Dreamstime/Fablic; 13 (bottom), Dreamstime/Fablic; 14, Dreamstime/Grybaz; 15, Dreamstime/Aniram; 17, Shutterstock/tele52; 18, Shutterstock/George Dolgikh; 19, Dreamstime/ Thayyilani; 20, Dreamstime/Pcruciatti; 21, Dreamstime/Tish; 22 Dreamstime/Aniram; 23, Dreamstime/Ongap; 24, Dreamstime/Nomadsoul1; 25, Dreamstime/Danieloizo; 26, Dreamstime/Cameronc; 27, Dreamstime/Vwstep; 28, Dreamstime/Auremar; 29, Dreamstime/Sprokop; cover (top left), Dreamstime/Aniram; cover (top right), Dreamstime/Tish; cover (bottom), Dreamstime/Pcruciatti.

Disclaimer

The website addresses (URLs) included in this book were valid at the time of going to press. However, because of the nature of the Internet, it is possible that some addresses may have changed, or sites may have changed or closed down since publication. While the author and Publisher regret any inconvenience this may cause the readers, no responsibility for any such changes can be accepted by either the author or Publisher.

CONTENTS

The world of ICT

Many of us study ICT at school and use it every day. ICT (Information and Communications Technology) refers to all the products that electronically store, retrieve, process, transmit and receive information or data. These products include computers, ranging from data-storing computers or servers to personal computers (PCs) and Macs, and the vast amount of software or programs used on them.

The first computers existed in offices and government departments from around the 1950s and 1960s, but ICT really spread from the 1980s onwards. This was because PCs became cheaper, and more people wanted to communicate using email and have access to the vast amount of information on the Internet.

↓ Some technology controlled by ICT, such as this robot that locates mines, carries out jobs that are very hazardous to people, and can even save lives.

↑ Modern communication technology allows people to stay in contact, even from remote places such as high mountain peaks.

What ICT has done for us

ICT is now used in almost every industry and in millions of businesses and homes worldwide. There are many examples of how ICT has transformed the world and reduced risks. For example, computer-controlled robots can be used to find landmines, paint cars and lay cables deep under the ocean, and in future they will be used to fight wars. ICT has also changed entertainment, for example through gaming and DVDs. Computer networks have connected individuals, businesses, organisations and nations, improving global communication, sales and the spread of ideas. ICT has also given us social networking through sites such as Facebook and Twitter.

Special skills

As you are reading this book, you are obviously good at ICT – maybe your parents think you even spend a little too much time on the computer! Skills that might come easily to you, such as problem-solving, thinking logically (approaching a problem step-by-step to find a solution), handling data and being patient, are useful in many ICT-related jobs and industries. This book introduces just a few.

Web designer

Playing games, viewing TV programmes, shopping and studying are just some of the reasons we visit websites, which are constructed by web designers. Websites are very important for businesses. For example, giant retailers such as Amazon and Ebay do not have shops on the high streets or in malls. They only sell products if people can find them easily on their websites. Governments, councils, schools, universities and charities are just some of the organisations that use websites to provide information.

– Job description –

Web designers:

- gather what is needed for the site (e.g. photos and text)
- check that each part has the right computer code so it shows up on the site properly
- decide on the style of lettering, colours, images and animations and arrange all the elements on the screen
- organise information on different pages within a site
- put in links between different pages
- upload websites onto servers
- pass on key information about the website to search engines such as Google so that people can find the site easily.

↓ Web designers develop the look of websites by coding different elements on each page.

What skills do I need?

Web design requires creativity and good computing skills. Designers need to be interested in the Internet and websites in general, in order to know what works and what doesn't. They need to be expert in using web-coding languages such as HTML and graphics software to help make logos and other parts of their design. Good communication skills and the ability to multi-task and work to tight deadlines are important. People often study web design at BTEC, City & Guilds or degree level, but it is really useful to learn coding languages via free tutorials on the Internet!

PROFESSIONAL VIEWPOINT

'There was a time when everyone was building their own websites... Now there is a realisation that the quality is substantially better when handed to professionals.'

Mary, web designer

Web designers need to work closely with website owners, writers and other people involved in creating effective websites.

Different types of web designer

Web designers often work closely with web writers who create the copy (text) for the site and account managers who liaise with clients over the purpose, audience and look they want for their websites. Some web designers work in one business or organisation. Others work on contracts for different clients as freelancers.

Recording engineer

Are you fussy about the music you listen to? Do you concentrate on the sound effects more than the visuals at the cinema? If so, you might like to become a recording engineer. Recording engineers are the people who record music, sound effects and speech for a wide range of media, from music CDs and websites to films, TV programmes and commercials.

Recording engineers often work closely with actors, musicians and sound effects specialists. The team leader is the producer. Producers may select songs to record, tell performers what to do during the recording session, and deal with the costs of recording.

→ Mixing desks look very complicated, but recording engineers learn to use them to make fine adjustments that improve the sounds audiences hear.

What skills do I need?

Recording engineering requires great patience and attention to detail. It is helpful to have an interest in new software and hardware, as the engineering process involves computer technology. You also need to have very good hearing, to be able to distinguish between different sounds. It is useful to have some musical skills, such as being able to tell if different musical tracks are in tune with each other or fit together with the same rhythm. You may need to work long hours at times when productions are on a tight schedule.

Different types of recording engineer

Some recording engineers work in recording studios. Others work in specialist post-production studios, where they process sound that has already been recorded elsewhere, such as underwater or in a jungle for a wildlife documentary. Others work at live gigs, concerts and festivals, recording the events.

Job description

Recording engineers:

- set up recording equipment, including positioning microphones near instruments to get the best sound
- record the sound using special tape machines or software
- use mixing desks to put separately recorded speech, music and effects tracks together into one master track
- use software to adjust the recorded tracks
- convert the master track into different digital formats.

Some recording engineers are skilled at positioning microphones in studios and at live performances in order to record the best possible sound from each instrument.

Database administrator

How can a doctor treat a patient without access to their medical records? How could weather forecasters do their job without data on weather patterns? How could a mail-order business survive without a list of people's addresses? Data may not sound like a very exciting area to work in, yet databases (or organised stores of data) are vital.

PROFESSIONAL VIEWPOINT
'You'll have to be the type to pay attention to detail and have a natural gift for organisation. If you like things just so, and have everything lined up in the right order, then it's a good option.'
Harrison, database administrator

Hard copy files are becoming a thing of the past in many businesses and organisations. Electronic files take up less space and can be organised, copied and 'backed-up' easily.

Different types of database administrator

There are many types of database administrator. Some work in hospitals or doctors' clinics, where they are responsible for clinical coding. This is typing in data for different patients, using standard codes. Clinically coded data include drugs taken and any allergies, hospital admissions and up-to-date contact details. The data aids treatment and also shows how much health services should charge governments or individuals for treatment. Some database administrators work for Internet-based retail businesses, such as Dell Computers or Amazon, for example ensuring that data about stock, prices or delivery dates is correct.

↑ Accurate and up-to-date data is important for many organisations and businesses, so the skills of database administrators are in demand.

What skills do I need?

Database administrators are usually methodical and have good literacy and ICT skills. Most have some interest in ICT developments so they can use the latest software to build and maintain databases effectively. For database administrators, inputting accurately and backing up their work is particularly important. Sometimes they need to be good at keeping secrets – some information is confidential so only certain people can access it. Database administrators usually have GCSEs/SCEs in English, maths and ICT, and some do apprenticeships or train while working as assistant administrators.

Graphic designer

Graphic designers often use pen tablets to create designs on-screen, as pen tablets give more control over lines than a computer mouse.

What do the characters on a cereal box, a poster advertising a new car, a holiday brochure and the branding on a football boot have in common? They are all the work of graphic designers.

Successful graphic designs are very memorable and can help to sell products or services. For example, the VW badge helps sell Volkswagen vehicles and the red I ♥ NY logo promotes tourism in New York City. Apple's iPhone, iPad and iPod are very popular modern technological devices. Their success is partly due to the work of graphic designers, whose use of smooth white casing, simple lettering styles and the Apple logo make the products so recognisable.

PROFESSIONAL VIEWPOINT

'Design is directed toward human beings. To design is to solve human problems by identifying them and executing the best solution.'

Ivan Chermayeff, graphic designer

Job description

Graphic designers:
- create visual identities for a wide range of products, services and activities
- choose different shapes and materials (e.g. in food packaging)
- make decisions on lettering and colour (e.g. on book or magazine covers)
- design the logos found on product labels.

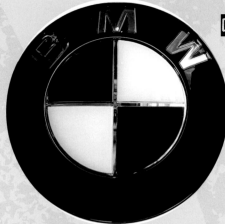

Graphic designers sometimes work just for one business or organisation, but mostly work for agencies that specialise in advertising design or business branding. To create a visual 'brand', they use distinctive combinations of colours, text, images and logos. Some graphic designers work full-time for particular companies but many are freelancers.

What skills do I need?

Graphic designers generally need to be skilled in using design software such as InDesign, Quark Xpress, FreeHand or Dreamweaver. These are standard tools used in different design companies. Most graphic designers are good at drawing and design, and will have studied art and graphic design at school. They often gain experience at college or university, but also while working in more junior jobs at agencies. They need to be able to master the use of software, and learn to create finished designs rapidly and to a high standard.

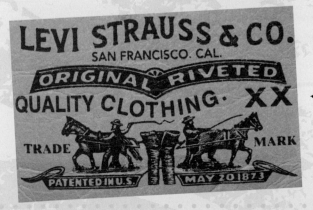

← Many of the familiar logos we see all around us are the work of graphic designers.

Telecommunications engineer

Have you ever thought about how much people rely on mobiles, landlines, email and Internet phones such as Skype to communicate with each other? This technology in turn relies on good networks of aerials, cables and satellites to work properly. Telecommunications engineers are the people who set up such networks and also invent, construct and spread new technologies for communication.

◀ It takes expertise to see past the jumble of wires and connect up complicated telecommunications equipment.

Different types of telecommunications engineer

Telecommunications engineers generally work for telephone and business network providers. These include call centres that provide telephone support for global businesses, as well as mobile phone companies such as Orange and T-Mobile. Engineers also work for digital and satellite TV companies, such as Sky, who offer their customers broadband and telephone subscriptions. There are many opportunities for telecommunications engineers – there are around 39,000 in the UK alone.

– Job description –

Telecommunications engineers:

• develop up-to-date telephone, messaging, cable, wireless and satellite communication technologies

• may have opportunities to work globally, especially if they work for a business that operates in many countries, such as Vodafone.

What skills do I need?

Telecommunications engineers usually study ICT, maths and sometimes sciences and business at school. Some have ICT or telecommunications engineering degrees, but others started off as apprentices within companies, sometimes on an IT and Telecoms Professionals Apprenticeship scheme. Once working in a company, most gain further qualifications to become recognised as Incorporated or Chartered Engineers. This recognised standard of ability is known worldwide.

The engineer's work varies depending on the employer. Some telecommunications engineers develop mobile phones that offer ever-improving technology, such as faster, more reliable Internet access. Others make sure that these technologies work with the existing networks of cables and aerial towers. Some are responsible for building new telecoms towers and dishes, or laying cables on the ground or under the oceans, to improve access to telecommunications for customers.

Some telecommunications engineers develop, set up and operate mobile phone masts so that mobile users with different networks can get a clear reception.

Software developer

Software contains the instructions that operate computers and other electronic devices in anything from fridges to fighter jets. People develop software for clients by writing a series of instructions in computer code. They either write new programs from scratch or take the cheaper option of adapting existing software to complete the task.

PROFESSIONAL VIEWPOINT

'It's the only job I can think of where I get to be both an engineer and an artist. There's an incredibly rigorous, technical element to it, which I like because you have to do very precise thinking. On the other hand, it has a wildly creative side where the boundaries of imagination are the only real limitation.'

Andy, software developer

Job description

Software developers:

- write code
- test software to make sure it works and fix any problems or bugs they discover
- train IT operators how to use the software properly
- work closely with different people such as business analysts (who work out what software is needed).

Software developers can create anything from simple interactive quizzes through to programs controlling complicated technology such as cars or power stations.

Different types of software developer

Software developers work in many industries, from banking and retail to engineering and education. Some software, such as Microsoft Windows, is widely available, and used on many computers. Other software is developed for more specialised use. For example, BlackBerry smart phones have software that allows phone users to personalise icons on their handset. In education, multimedia interactive software is developed to enhance learning for individuals. Depending on the individual's response, the software may explain concepts differently and provide different amounts of information to suit their abilities.

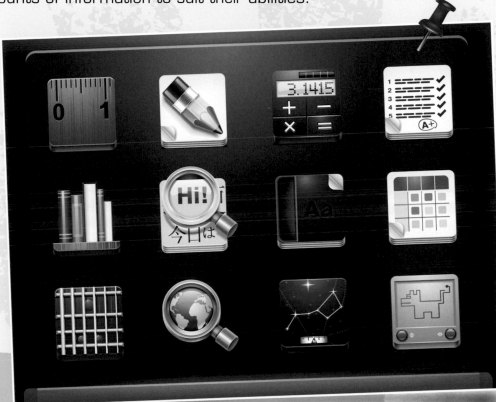

These are icons found on some interactive whiteboards. They link to fun and stimulating educational software for children.

What skills do I need?

The most useful skill is fluency in one or several programming languages, such as SQL, Java and Visual Basic. Many programmers become interested in writing in code at school, and usually take ICT and computing courses at college and university. Software developers need to be precise in their writing and patient enough to solve any bugs. They also need to communicate well in order to understand what clients want, and to express their solutions in English as well as code!

IT technical sales specialist

Are you interested in computer developments? Do you know enough about computers to advise others on what they need to buy? Then you might like to become an IT technical sales specialist. These people use their knowledge to sell the hardware (including computers, hard drives and printers) and software products produced by IT and software businesses. Typical businesses employing technical sales specialists include Apple stores and online computer sellers such as Dell.

PROFESSIONAL VIEWPOINT

'You have to listen to people: the client, the people who make the products, other users – to everyone, in fact, so that you can take into account all the information and propose the right technical solution. So you need "people" skills, technical knowledge, common sense, and a certain feeling for selling.'

Claire, IT sales

Job description

IT technical sales specialists:

- find out what the customer needs
- try to find products matching the customers' requirements
- demonstrate products and see if anything needs to be improved, for example by adding anti-virus software
- answer any technical questions from clients and make sure they are happy with the systems they have chosen.

↑ A trained technical sales specialist team can deal with any questions, and assist customers in choosing the right ICT systems.

The Acer Computers sales centre at the GITEX Technology Week exhibition in Dubai. Exhibitions like this provide opportunities for technical sales specialists to meet customers and sell them the latest products.

A technical sales specialist typically asks clients questions about their computing and system requirements to make sure they buy the right thing. For example, they might ask: Do you want a powerful computer for gaming or an office computer that can be fitted into a network easily? How much can you afford to spend on each computer?

What skills do I need?

To become an IT technical sales specialist you obviously need to be able to sell things! Often the specialist will need to negotiate or haggle over prices, especially for large sales such as new computers for a large office. You will usually be interested in hardware and software developments, including technical details, and have preferences about different products. Sometimes you might need to make presentations about your recommendations to clients. Technical sales specialists sometimes have BTEC Higher National or degree qualifications in computer science/IT, but others gain the technical expertise they need from selling computers in shops or online businesses. Some specialists manage teams or run consultancies working for a range of businesses, either within companies or as freelancers.

Games designer

If you marvel at the virtual worlds created in famous games such as Halo or World of Warcraft then you might like to become a computer games designer. Games are not just for entertainment. They are also used to help with training. For example, trainee pilots learn how to fly aeroplanes with flight simulator games, operated by the real equipment a pilot would have in a real plane. Some games can even help people get healthy. These include Wii fitness games and special games designed to help young people make better choices, such as eating healthily or avoiding drugs.

Job description

Games designers:
- devise and design new games
- work from their own or from other people's original ideas
- come up with the rules of the game
- design the characters, the settings and the objects used in the game.

↓ Some games designers create incredibly realistic car rallying or racing games that make players feel as if they are really driving a car at high speed.

Many children's computer games revolve around the adventures of cartoon characters developed by games designers. →

Different types of games designer

Designers usually work in games businesses. In small companies, designers may do all the programming themselves. In big games companies, such as Nintendo or Bungie, there might be separate design and programming departments, in which some people will specialise, for instance, in making a particular character move smoothly or creating imaginative backgrounds. A big project, such as a new blockbuster game, might take a large team months and lots of money to develop.

PROFESSIONAL VIEWPOINT
'Look real hard at your idea. Hunt the web and figure out how cheap the games you'll be competing with are. When you are sure you want to write a game that you can get people to buy, only then should you proceed.'
Jeff, games designer

What skills do I need?

Most games designers are graduates in design and IT subjects. They are expert in using computer coding languages such as C++, and many start to use these at school. Designers are usually good at solving problems, working in teams, and adapting quickly to the demands of the public and of games companies. Most importantly, they must love gaming. Some move into the role of designer after working as games testers – people whose job is to play games and suggest improvements before they are released for sale.

IT services worker

When workers in a business need to clear a virus off their computer or make their email work, or if they have problems with their work computer server, they usually call IT services. Without IT service workers, many organisations might grind to a halt because they rely so much on IT systems!

↑ An ICT technician may be asked to do anything from installing software on to a laptop to mending the fan inside a PC.

Different types of IT service worker

In small companies, one person might look after IT services, but in large organisations there are often different types of IT service worker. For example, ICT technicians make sure that hardware and software work properly. Their work ranges from mending broken keyboards to setting up complex communication systems for the RAF and other armed forces. Network managers or administrators install networks of cables and servers containing data for multiple users. These networks provide shared access to files, email and the Internet, as well as printers, and may be local, national or even global.

Job description

IT service workers:
- set up IT systems in a business or organisation
- maintain the IT systems
- solve any IT problems.

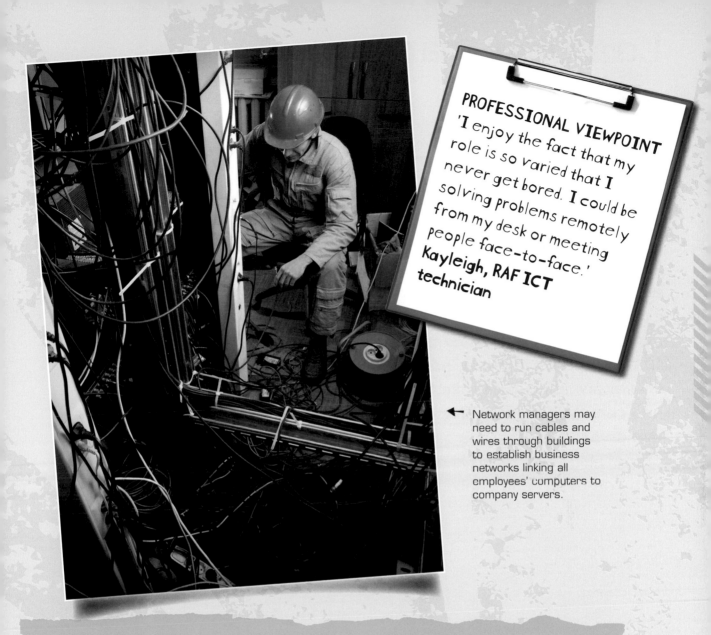

← Network managers may need to run cables and wires through buildings to establish business networks linking all employees' computers to company servers.

What skills do I need?

To work in IT services, you will usually need good GCSEs/SCEs in ICT, science, English and maths. Further training varies according to the type of service work you want to do. For example, RAF technicians train at the RAF Radio School, and network managers often have degrees in IT and/or business and years of experience in order to oversee important networks. IT service skills are useful in many different industries and countries, and there are opportunities to work in a single organisation or in several as a freelancer. However, you must be prepared to work early in the morning, at weekends and evenings – these are the best times to install or mend networks without interrupting other workers!

Computer hardware engineer

Do you like to take computers apart or customise computers to get the best specifications? Computer hardware engineers work on both mechanical and electronic computer parts or components. Mechanical components include sliding CD or DVD trays, fans to cool electronic parts, hard drives that store information, keyboards and remote controls. Electronic components include the central processing unit, which is the 'brain' of a computer, and cabling.

Hardware engineers may supervise the careful production of processors in specialised factories to ensure that the processors work perfectly.

Different types of computer hardware engineer

Many different industries employ computer hardware engineers. Some work for component makers such as Intel, computer system manufacturers such as IBM or telecommunications companies. Others work in the financial, retail and leisure industries, creating anything from banking systems to lottery ticket machines and mechanisms for talking toys.

Job description

Computer hardware engineers:

- design and develop computers
- use software to design microchips and other computer components
- design and develop computerised components for other appliances, such as car engine management systems and hi-fi or home cinema systems
- create prototypes of new components for manufacture
- assemble existing components into new systems
- test their designs to make sure the finished product works as it should.

What skills do I need?

Hardware engineers are usually very practical, with a lot of scientific and technical know-how and good awareness of current computer technology. They need to keep up-to-date with developments in computing because these happen so fast! Good communication skills are important in order to understand what hardware people require from computer systems. After studying maths, ICT and physics at school, would-be hardware engineers may become IT/ telecommunications apprentices working at a computer manufacturer. Others get BTECs or degrees in computer or electronic engineering before starting work. On these advanced courses, they will learn skills including how to use hardware design software such as VHDL.

↓ Many of the miniature circuits and microprocessors controlling electronic devices, from TVs to washing machines, are designed by hardware engineers.

Animator

Are you good at IT and also love to draw? Are you a fan of films with spectacular animation, from **Avatar** to **Wall-E**? Animators create sequences of images (frames) that appear to move on screen. To become an animator, qualifications are very important, but it is also vital to show others how well you animate by making a showreel. This is like a video CV of short, varied pieces of work, such as sequences of characters walking, balls bouncing or clouds moving.

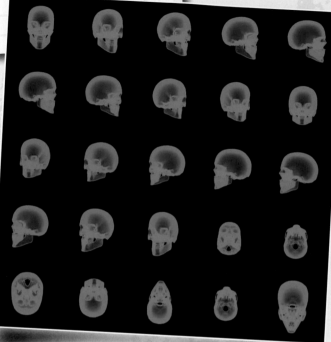

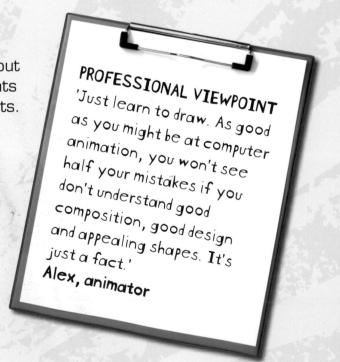

↑ Animation is not just for entertainment but also for education. For example, animated skeletons can help medical students understand human anatomy.

Different types of animator

Some animators work on feature films but others produce short animated segments for websites, or for TV or cinema adverts. Some carry out all the tasks needed to make a film, including writing a script, planning and drawing frames, and adding sound. Others have particular roles in teams in large animation studios such as Pixar or Disney. For example, keyframers draw important frames that are vital to tell the story in the film, and tweeners fill in the gaps between them.

PROFESSIONAL VIEWPOINT

'Just learn to draw. As good as you might be at computer animation, you won't see half your mistakes if you don't understand good composition, good design and appealing shapes. It's just a fact.'

Alex, animator

Animators:

- draw and use specialised computer software to create sequences of frames
- put together frames with music and sound effects
- edit films and create finished products.

↓ Computer software is used to edit animated sequences, together with soundtracks, into completed films. Sometimes the editing process requires several computer screens to accurately visualise and tie together all the elements of a film.

What skills do I need?

Many animators studied art as well as ICT at school or college, and have a degree or HNC/HND in animation or graphic design. Animators need creativity and imagination. They should take an interest in how things move realistically, so they can try to imitate this in animation. Animators also need great patience – it can take a week to draw frames that fill only three seconds on screen! Knowledge of 3D software will be essential in many animation jobs. Some of the software is very complicated, but you can learn the principles by using simpler programs such as Poser or Amorphium in your spare time. Possibly the most important skill is drawing, so practise as much as you can.

IT trainer

PROFESSIONAL VIEWPOINT

'I believe that the role of the trainer is to help people to work out the answer for themselves. It's the "wow" moment – "Wow, I didn't know I could do that!" – that makes me continue to be a trainer. You've done a good job if they don't need you any more!'

Michelle, IT trainer

Do you like to show others how software works, and pass on your computer knowledge? An IT trainer teaches people how to use information and communications technology. This includes the use of software packages and hardware such as PCs, laptops and interactive whiteboards. Good trainers plan lessons carefully so they do not teach people too fast or too slowly. They constantly check how well people are learning so that they can create more effective training programmes.

↓ Some IT trainers work in school or college settings, teaching younger people how to use software and hardware in their studies.

Other IT trainers may address large audiences about commercial IT products, as shown here at an international conference on satellite navigation products.

Different types of IT trainer

Some IT trainers teach others about commercially available software, such as Microsoft Excel, or how to set up firewall hardware for computers. Some train people in how to use specialist software for organisations, such as clinical coding software (see pages 10–11). Others may teach people in businesses how to use social networking sites, including Facebook, to advertise their goods or services.

Trainers may teach very different audiences. These range from seminars for large groups of professionals in big organisations, such as banks, to computer basics classes for pensioners in night school or prisoners in jail. Some trainers work almost entirely on Internet-based training programmes.

What skills do I need?

Most importantly, you must want to teach others. This requires both excellent IT understanding and also communication skills, in order to deliver your courses to different groups in the most effective ways. You will need to be able to capture people's interest and express complicated ideas in simple ways. Many trainers have computing or business degrees, but others have widely recognised qualifications such as the European Computer Driving Licence (ECDL).

Job description

IT trainers:
- analyse the training needs in a business or organisation by assessing the ICT abilities of staff
- develop and deliver appropriate training programmes
- use a mix of classroom and practical exercises
- work full-time in organisations or as freelancers.

Glossary

aerial device that sends or receives radio and television signals

agency business or organisation that provides a particular service, e.g. an advertising agency

anti-virus something that finds and destroys computer viruses

apprenticeship time spent working for an employer to learn skills needed for a job

branding giving a name and image to goods or services to interest people in them

bug fault in a computer system or program

charity organisation that helps people, environments or animals in need

code system of words, numbers, letters or symbols that represent a message or record information

data facts or information stored by a computer

database organised set of data stored in a computer

digital system of sending and receiving information using a series of Os and 1s

electronic device that works by using electric signals

firewall system that stops other people gaining access to files on your computer

freelancer person who works for several different organisations rather than just one

hard copy printed version of something on a computer

hardware machinery and electronic parts of a computer system

interactive when information passes to and fro between a computer and the person using it

Internet worldwide system of interconnected networks and computers

logically based on facts or sensible reasons

logo symbol or picture that a company uses as its special sign

microchip small computer part that stores computer memory

microphone device for recording sounds

network number of computers connected together so they can share information

process to perform a series of operations on a computer

producer person who arranges for someone to make something such as a CD or a TV show

programming language language designed for writing instructions for computers

script written text of a computer program, a film or a play

server computer program that controls or supplies information to several computers connected in a network

software programs used to operate a computer

virus instructions hidden in a computer program that are designed to cause faults or destroy data in the computer

website part of the Internet where an organisation or individual puts information

Further information

There are many specific courses, apprenticeships and jobs using ICT skills, so where do you go to find out more? It is really useful to meet up with careers advisers at school or college and to attend careers fairs to see the range of opportunities. Remember that public libraries and newspapers are other important sources of information. The earlier you check out your options, the better prepared you will be to put your ICT skills to good use as you earn a living in future.

Books

Career Building Through Interactive Online Games (Digital Career Building), Meg Swaine, Rosen Publishing, 2007

Career Ideas for Kids Who Like Computers (Career Ideas for Kids), Diane Lindsey Reeves, Facts On File Inc, 2007

Careers in Computer Gaming (Cutting-Edge Careers), Matthew Robinson, Rosen Publishing, 2007

Computer Game Developer (Weird Careers in Science), Mary Firestone, Chelsea House Publishers, 2005

Computers (Discovering Careers for Your Future) Infobase Publishing, Facts On File Inc, 2008

Game Programming for Teens, Maneesh Seti, Delmar Publishing, 2008

Websites

www.prospects.ac.uk/options_computer_science_it_your_skills.htm
This website is a useful guide to your job options. It is aimed at IT graduates and it gives a clear idea of what routes to take for ICT careers. There is also a comprehensive list of resources and contacts on this site.

archives.igda.org/breakingin/career_paths.htm
Do you want to have a career in games? Find out more by visiting this website and following the links to audio, design, production and other aspects of putting computer games together.

www.saludos.com/fields/compeng.html
Visit this website to find out about careers in computing and/or engineering.

www.yournxtstep.co.uk/ict.html
This website has some useful ICT career profiles.

computingcareers.acm.org/?page_id=4
Find out the top 10 reasons to study computing at university, with this IT degrees and careers website. It covers everything from 'skills you'll learn' to 'what computing professionals do'.

www.wetfeet.com/Careers-and-Industries/Careers/Information-Technology.aspx
A useful summary of IT career requirements, career tracks, and the state of the global job market.

Index

I'M GOOD AT...

Contents of all the titles in the series:

WAYLAND